Published by Creative Education
123 South Broad Street, Mankato, Minnesota 56001
Creative Education is an imprint of The Creative Company

Designed by Stephanie Blumenthal
Production Design by Melinda Belter

Photographs by Frank Balthis, Corbis, Richard Cummins, Grace Davies,
GeoIMAGERY (Bill Webster, Bob Grytton), David Liebman, Craig Lovell, Erwin C.
"Bud" Nielson/Images International, Rory Prodoehl, Rainbow, Cheryl Richter, Inga
Spence, Tom Stack and Associates, Sally Weigand, Ingrid Marn Wood

Library of Congress Cataloging-in-Publication Data

Healy-Johnson, Guinevere, 1967–
Cotton / by Guinevere Healy-Johnson
p. cm. — (Let's Investigate)
Includes glossary
Summary: Briefly describes how cotton is grown, the pests and fungi that
threaten it, and how it is processed into various types of fabrics.
ISBN 0-88682-959-3
1. Cotton—Juvenile literature. 2. Cotton growing—Juvenile literature. 3. Cotton
manufacture—Juvenile literature [1. Cotton.] I. Title. II. Series. III. Series:
Let's Investigate (Mankato, Minn.)
SB249.H435   1999
633.5'1—dc21   98-13013

First edition

2 4 6 8 9 7 5 3 1

COTTON

GUINEVERE HEALY-JOHNSON

Creative C Education

COTTON
SPACE

Cotton was the fabric chosen to make the in-flight space suits worn by the space shuttle astronauts.

Above, cotton is used for cloth baby diapers Center, cotton fabric

The United States raises many crops, from corn to wheat to sugar. Few crops are as useful in so many ways as cotton. Not only does cotton provide us with clothing, it also gives us a wide variety of products, from cooking oil to bandages to couch cushions. It provides hundreds of thousands of jobs for people working on farms, in factories, and in stores, and we rely on it every day, probably without even realizing it.

COTTON
COLOR

India "madras" is a coarse, hand-loomed fabric that is often colored with vegetable dyes. These dyes are washed almost completely out, leaving the fabric a pale color.

6

Below, cotton turban
Center, harvesting cotton

GROWING COTTON

Cotton comes from a plant, so it is called a natural fiber. Some other **textile** materials are wool and silk, which come from animals. These are called animal fibers. Synthetic fibers are not natural, nor do they come from animals. They are **man-made** fibers. Of all these kinds of fibers, cotton is often thought to make the most comfortable and lightweight clothing.

Cotton grows primarily in the warm lands of the southern and south-western United States. This area, known as the "Cotton Belt," runs from northern Florida up to Virginia and back west to California. Large cotton farms are found in Texas, California, the Missis-sippi River valley, and southern Arizona.

Around the world, cotton is grown in 70 countries. China pro-duces the most—more than 25 percent of all the cotton grown in the world. The United States produces almost 20 per-cent of the world's total.

COTTON
DESERT

Muslin is one of the first cotton fabrics; it was first woven in Iraq, where people made lightweight clothing for life in desert regions.

COTTON
TREES

Catechu is a brown dye that is made by boiling small bits of wood from the acacia tree; adding certain metals to the mixture adds yellow or green to the brown color.

COTTON
WARTIME

In the early 1800s, when the infamous leader Napoleon waged war on Britain and cut off its silk **imports,** *people had to make thread from cotton—and soon decided they liked it better than silk!*

Above, hibiscus
Right, young cotton

The cotton plant belongs to the same plant family as hibiscus (a flower) and okra (a vegetable). Of the 30 different species, or kinds, of cotton, only three are farmed. One species, *Gossypium hirsutum,* makes up about 90 percent of the cotton grown worldwide. In the U.S., cotton is planted in the spring and harvested in the late summer and early fall. A cotton plant is a little tree three to six feet (1–2 m) tall.

The plant adapts well to poor soil, but it needs a lot of sunlight and water. In areas where little rain falls, farmers use **irrigation** systems to bring water to their land.

Weeds are killed with **herbicides** and a process called "flaming." As cotton plants grow, their stems harden. At this time the field can be "flamed," or burned with a quick burst of fire that kills weeds but doesn't hurt the cotton plants.

Mature cotton

COTTON
WEAPON

*Guncotton was an **explosive** invented by Christian Shonbein in 1845. It was made by mixing cotton with various acids, but it proved to be too dangerous to use!*

COTTON
A R T

Batik (buh-TEEK) is a cloth made by pouring hot wax over fabric in a pattern and then dyeing the cloth. The dye doesn't soak into the wax, so a pattern is left on the cloth when the wax is lifted.

Above, batik fabrics
Right, cotton square

As the plants grow, they produce little buds, called "squares." These buds bloom into flowers that start out creamy white or yellow and change to pink or dark red. As time passes, the flower falls off, leaving a tiny pod-like growth. This pod, shaped like a football, is where the cotton fibers will grow.

In a month or two, the pod breaks open into a "cotton boll." This pure white fluffy fiber is the beginning of cotton as we know it. The long white seed hairs on the cotton plant are called "lint." They cover up many black or brown seeds. Lint, and shorter fibers called "linters," are attached to the seeds.

COTTON
A R M Y

Various species of ants are often encouraged to live in cotton fields, where they attack and eat other, sometimes bigger, insects that are harmful to the cotton plants.

COTTON
S P I N N I N G

In 14th-century Europe, the spinning wheel was invented, making the process of turning cotton and wool into yarn much faster and easier.

Open cotton boll

COTTON
ARTWORK

Artists' canvas is tightly woven, heavy fabric most often made of cotton; it is specially treated to hold on to the paint that is spread over its surface.

Above, Guatemalan woman weaving dyed cotton yarn
Right, caterpillars are destructive to cotton

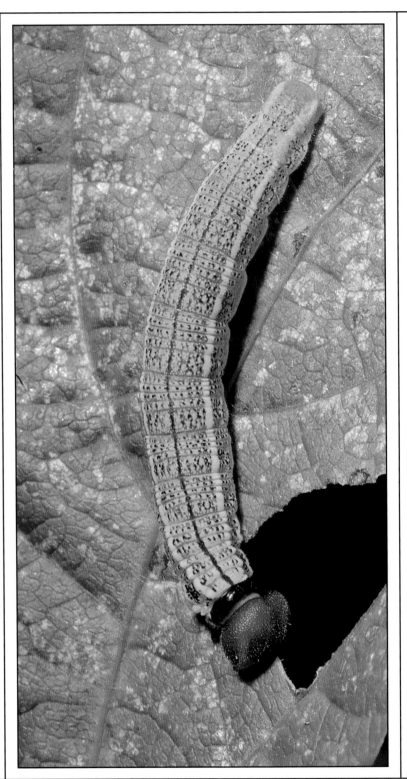

DANGERS TO COTTON

Cotton is a hardy plant, but insects, **fungi,** and harsh weather can threaten its growth. Cotton thrives on sunlight and moisture, but too much rainfall can ruin plants. Heavy rains turn cotton a dirty gray color instead of its usual clean white.

At one time the flag of Uzbekistan, in Central Asia, had cotton bolls on it, which symbolized harmony and successful farming.

This color change lowers the **grade** of the cotton. Hard rains can decrease the amount of cotton harvested, and high moisture can allow damaging **mold** to spread. Too much rain can also make it difficult or impossible to get farm machinery into the muddy fields. All of these problems can mean less money paid to the farmers for their crops.

Left, spiders eat insect pests

COTTON
GROUP

14

Spraying pesticide

Insects are another danger. The cotton flowers and leaves hold **nectar,** something that many insects love to eat. The *boll weevil,* a type of beetle, is especially harmful. Boll weevils lay their eggs inside the cotton boll. When the young eat their way out, the plant is killed.

Pesticides help to control boll weevils, but the bugs can become **resistant** and hard to control. In addition, the pesticides often kill many other bugs that can actually be helpful to cotton because they eat the boll weevils.

*B*ollworms, the pink larvae, or young, of a moth, are also difficult to control. Soon after hatching from their eggs, the larvae burrow into the cotton bolls. Pesticides don't always reach them in time to save the plants. The *bollworm-tobacco budworm* attacks both cotton and another southern crop—**tobacco** plants. *Armyworms* and *red spiders* also attack cotton. Farmers must take care to control these insects while at the same time ensuring the safety of the plants and the environment.

COTTON
WHEELS

In the early 20th century, when the first automobiles were built, the tires were made of cotton cloth that had been coated with rubber.

Right, boll weevil trap

COTTON
MUMMIES

Mummies, the preserved bodies of people who have died, were made thousands of years ago. In ancient Peru, mummies were wrapped in cotton.

Right, cotton harvester
Opposite, raw cotton

Some fungi enter the cotton plant's roots from the soil and poison the plant. Another fungus called *anthracnose*, or boll rot, gets into the cotton plant's **sac.** This stops the growth of the boll and eventually chokes the plant. To control fungi, wilt-resistant varieties of cotton plants have been developed, and seeds that are not infected with fungus are used to plant fields.

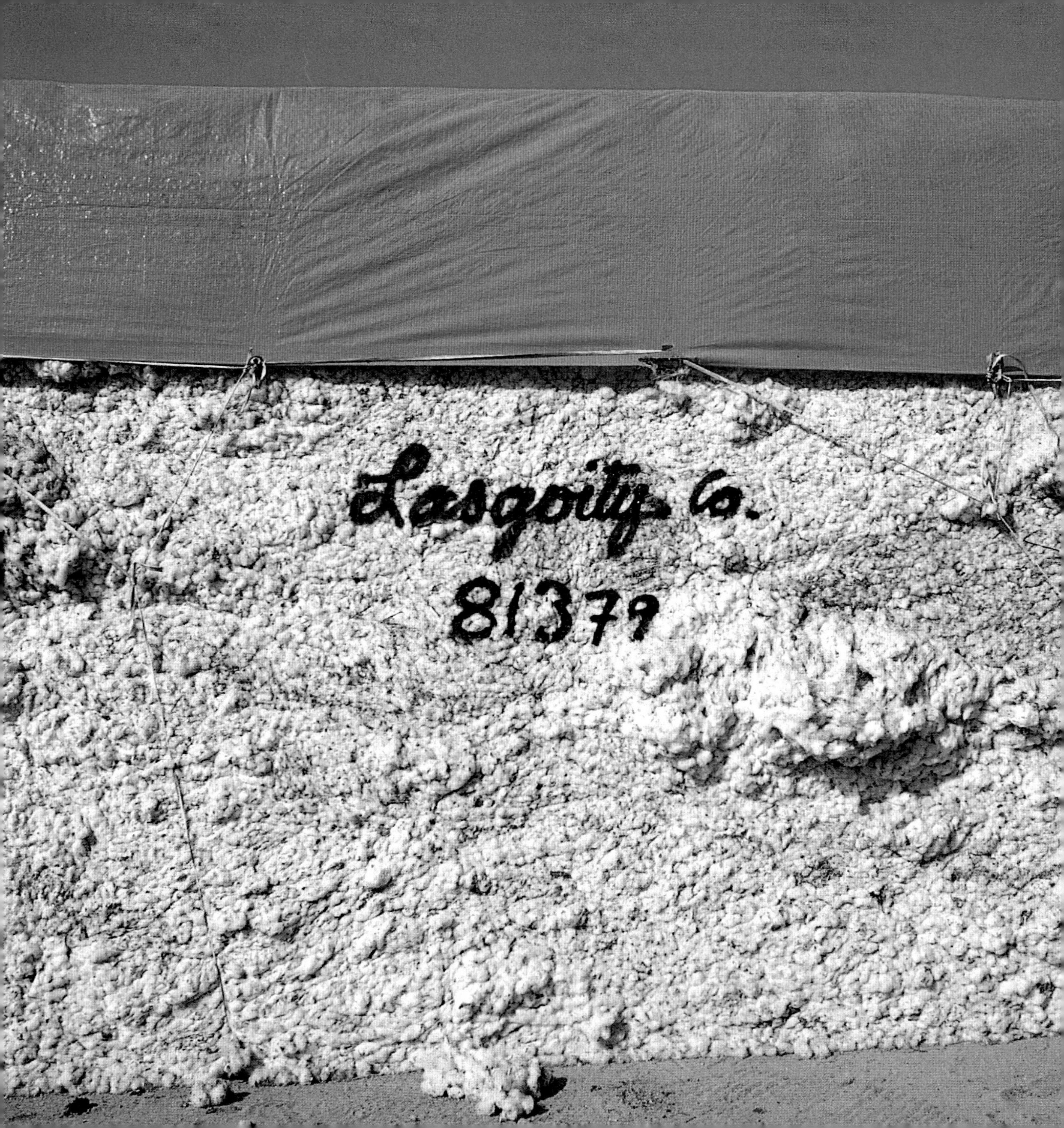
Lasgoity Co.
81379

COTTON
FACTORY

In 1813, Francis Cabot Lowell built the world's first factory that could make cotton yarn as well as cloth all in one building. The factory was in Waltham, Massachusetts.

COTTON
DANGER

Years ago, workers in textile mills sometimes developed "brown lung," a disease caused by inhaling cotton dust; the result was difficulty in breathing.

Cotton in a gin

COTTON PROCESSING

After cotton is harvested, it is taken to the gin. The first cotton gin was invented by Eli Whitney in 1793. The machine, which ran on steam power, provided a fast, easy method for separating cotton into its various parts. Before this invention, the seeds had to be picked out by hand, which was a slow, tiring job. The cotton gin made cotton production much easier for people.

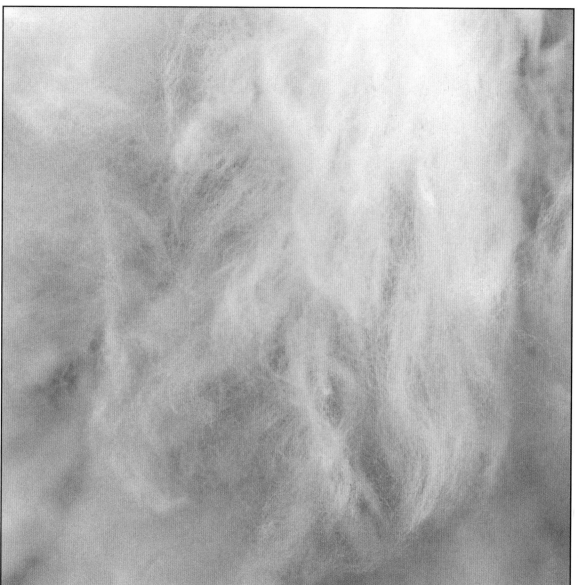

Fabric brighteners or bleaches, also called fluorescent whitening agents, or FWAs, are absorbed especially well by fabrics made of natural cotton.

Left, close view of ginned cotton Above, cotton fleecewear

Today, cotton is processed in factories using even faster machines run on electricity. The cotton is pulled through powerful pipes into a dryer. Cleaning machines then remove stems, leaves, burrs, dirt, and other foreign material from the parts of the cotton that will be used. The cleaned cotton next moves to the gin stand, where sharp saws tear the cotton fibers from the seeds.

QUESTION

*What can be made
from one 500-pound
bale of cotton?*

ANSWER

*250 pairs of pants
409 skirts
690 bath towels
1,256 pillow cases
3,085 diapers
or
4,321 socks*

*Below, cotton seeds
Right, baled cotton*

Some of the cotton seeds are saved to plant the next year's crop. Other cotton seeds are smashed in crushing mills for their oil. Cottonseed oil is an ingredient in many items such as cooking and salad oils, margarine, and snack foods. Some products contain the crushed seed hulls. These include floor covering, animal feed, and **fertilizer.**

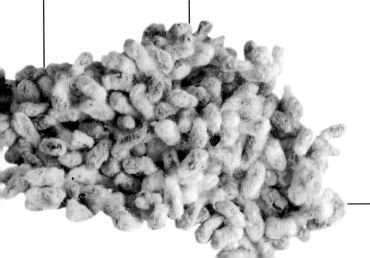

Even the tiny linters are used. They make good mattress stuffing, and even paper and X-ray film. The longer fibers—the lint—are pressed into bales that weigh about 500 pounds each. Some cotton gins can process as many as 60 of these bales in one hour. Workers separate each bale into different grades. They judge the cleanliness, color, length, and fineness of the fibers. The bales are then either **exported** to other countries or taken to a textile mill to be made first into yarn and then into cloth.

COTTON
PICKIN'

Cotton was once harvested by hand, but machines can now pick cotton 50 times faster than a person could pick.

COTTON
FACT

Cotton is used for many different products, but more than half of the cotton used in the U.S. is made into clothing.

COTTON
NEEDLES

Knitting machines may use as many as 2,500 needles at once to knit different colored threads into fancy fabric prints and designs.

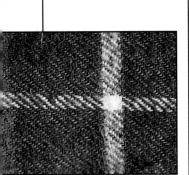

Above, cotton flannel Right and far right, marbleized paper made with cotton fibers

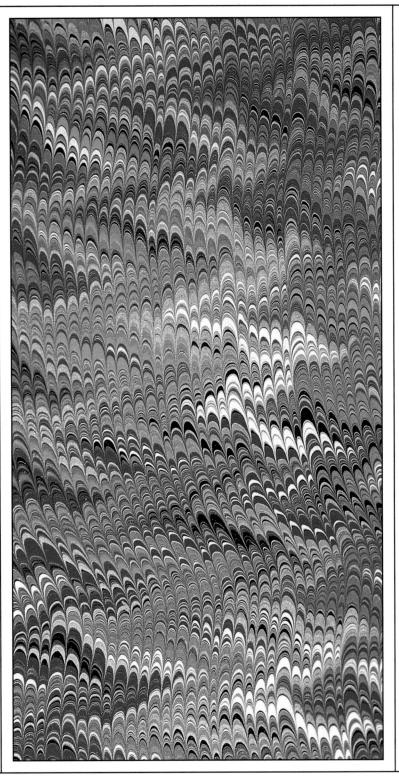

At the textile mill, machines open the bales. The lint is mixed up and cleaned again with beaters and blowers. The best parts of the lint are the longer strands—those between one and two inches (2.5–5 cm) in length. Shorter strands are saved as well, for use in such products as paper, cotton balls, stuffings for toys, and typewriter ribbons.

The bundles of fluffy cotton are sent to a "carding" machine. This cleans the fibers again.

It lays the fibers side by side in a thin sheet, or web. Then the fibers are pulled through a funnel-like device that makes them into a soft rope called a **sliver.** A "drawing frame" pulls out six slivers and twists them into one. From there the thick rope is twisted tighter and pulled into a thinner rope. Finally, the slivers move to a spinning machine, where they are pulled and twisted still tighter into yarn. Yarn can be made to any length and thickness, depending on the type of textile being made.

COTTON
VALUE

Calico is one of the oldest fabrics made from cotton. It originated in Calicut, India, and because it was quite beautiful it became valuable to Europeans.

23

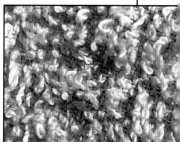

Above, cotton terry

COTTON

In 1849, a man named Levi Strauss made his fortune by inventing and producing cotton denim jeans, which he called Levi's.

COTTON

Textile art was made famous in the Far East thousands of years ago. Beautiful cotton wall hangings, called "noren," are still made today.

Right, cotton-tipped swabs
Opposite, cotton thread

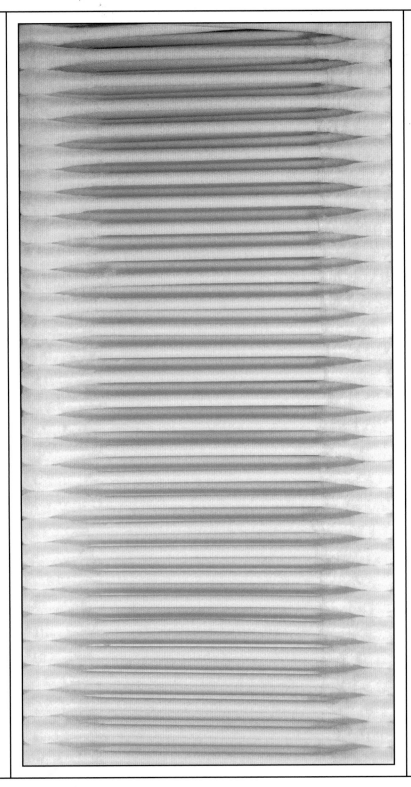

Massive rolls of thin cotton threads can be knitted into the cloth used to make underwear, T-shirts, socks, and other light clothing items. Some cotton fibers can also be pressed tightly to make cheap, paperlike fabrics used for notebooks, workbooks, and some kinds of paper.

COTTON
INVENTION

After trying more than 1,000 different materials, inventor Thomas Edison used burned cotton to make a part for the world's very first electric light.

Above, cotton yarn
Right, denim blue jeans

MAKING FABRIC

More than 120 different types of fabric, from blue-jean denim to pajama flannel, can be made from cotton. The large machines that weave cotton yarns into various fabrics are called looms. The first looms were operated by hand hundreds of years ago. The way they work has not changed much over the years, but modern machine-driven looms are much faster. The weaving process is quite simple. Rows of yarn, called the "warp," are positioned vertically (up and down) on the loom. Yarn called the "filling" are interlocked with the warp by running horizontally (side to side) on the loom. These first pieces of woven fabric are called "gray goods."

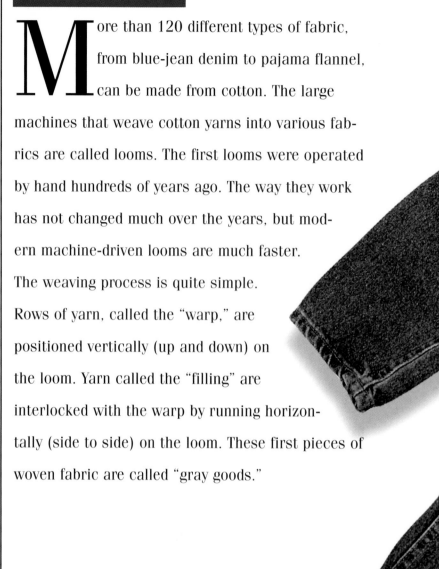

A species of red cotton

The fabric is then sold to "converters," people who further prepare the fabric for market. Many different methods are used to process a fabric. The gray goods can be bleached, dyed, preshrunk, or printed, depending on the type of fabric and pattern that is wanted. Special finishings, such as waterproofing and stain protection, are used to improve the usefulness and **durability** of some garments and furnishings.

COTTON

KABOOM

Cotton linters are used as filler material in some explosives, and cotton fibers are sometimes used for fuses on firecrackers and sticks of dynamite.

COTTON

MUSEUM

The American Cotton Museum in Greenville, Texas, has artifacts and exhibits that show historic activities in the Texas cotton business.

*Right, old-fashioned spinning wheel
Below, mummy*

HISTORY OF COTTON

No one knows when or where the first cotton was processed, but scientists have found boll pieces in Mexico that are 7,000 years old. Cotton has been used in Pakistan and India for 5,000 years. The ancient Egyptians, Chinese, and **indigenous** peoples of North and South America also raised cotton.

As early as 1607, settlers in the Jamestown Colony, Virginia, the first colony in the United States, planted cotton. Although the first crop failed, the people kept trying, and soon cotton production grew throughout the Cotton Belt. Over the years, farmers and textile mills have continually improved their methods. Better methods of planting, growing, and production have made cotton a huge industry. By the mid-1990s, about 20 million tons (18 metric tons) of cotton were being grown each year.

The boll weevil, one of cotton's most dangerous threats, is only about the size of a pencil eraser.

A loom for weaving cotton rugs

COTTON

BLUE

Indigo, the blue dye used to color denim and other cotton fabrics, is thousands of years old. It first came from the leaves of the Indigofera plant, but today it is man-made.

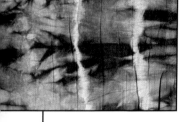

Above, indigo-dyed cotton fabric Right, cotton field in Arizona

Cotton grows all over the world, wherever there is sunshine and just the right amount of rain. It provides jobs for people on farms, in factories, and in stores that sell cotton products. With so many uses, from paper to food to clothes, cotton is sure to remain one of the world's most valuable natural **resources.**

Glossary

When something is tough and able to withstand wear and tear, it is said to have **durability.**

An **explosive** is something that explodes, or blows up.

Goods and products made one by country and sold to another country are said to be **exported.**

Fertilizer is something that helps plants grow faster and stronger; it can be a man-made substance, or it can be natural, such as animal manure.

Fungi may look like plants, but they are not exactly plants; they grow where it is moist, and some kinds can be harmful to plants. Mushrooms and molds are types of fungi.

The **grade** is the class of cotton that ranges from very good to just okay.

Herbicides are man-made substances, sprayed on fields in liquid or powder form, that are used to kill weeds.

Imports are the opposite of exports; they are goods purchased by one country that were originally made by a different country.

A person, plant, or animal that is originally from an area or region is said to be **indigenous** to that place.

Irrigation systems supply water to land that is dry; water can be pumped through long pipes from large wells or even rivers and lakes.

Anything that is **man-made** is made by humans and is not naturally occurring.

Mold is a fungus (the singular of fungi); it is a fuzzy growth than can ruin plants.

The sweet liquid that is produced by flowers and some plants is called **nectar;** many insects eat nectar.

Pesticides are similar to herbicides, but these substances are used to kill bugs.

When an insect becomes stronger and is no longer affected by a pesticide that is intended to kill it, the insect has become **resistant** to the pesticide.

Resources are things, either natural or man-made, that can be used for some valuable purpose.

A **textile** is anything that was made by weaving or knitting; cloth is a textile.

The **tobacco** plant is grown widely in the southern United States; its leaves are dried and made into cigarettes.

A cotton plant has a **sac** underneath the boll. When fungi invade the sac, the boll stops growing; then the plant weakens and dies.

A **sliver** (SLY-ver) is a rope of cotton before it is finished.

Index